Dear Christmas Carol Singer,

    For over two decades our family hosted about 100 people on the Sunday before Christmas for our annual Carol Singing. It was a wonderful experience to enjoy family, friends and food while celebrating the birth of Jesus.

    Singers and non-singers alike looked forward to this Christmas tradition. For most songs, everyone sung together in unison. Other times, the old crooners sang for the group, or the younger singers serenaded everyone. Every year there were a few talented soloists or musicians who came prepared to display their vocal and musical abilities.

    Singing this compilation of traditional Christmas carols, hymns and popular songs, brought us immeasurable joy through the years. Our hope is that it will do the same for your family and friends.

From our family to yours,

The Grant family

Table of Contents

ANGELS FROM THE REALMS OF GLORY..1

ANGELS WE HAVE HEARD ON HIGH..2

AS WITH GLADNESS MEN OF OLD..3

AWAY IN A MANGER...4

CHRISTIANS AWAKE..5

DECK THE HALLS..6

GO TELL IT ON THE MOUNTAIN...7

GOD REST YE MERRY GENTLEMEN...8

GOOD CHRISTIAN MEN REJOICE...9

GOOD KING WENCESLAS...10

HARK! THE HERALD ANGELS SING...11

I HEARD THE BELLS ON CHRISTMAS DAY..12

I SAW THREE SHIPS..13

IT CAME UPON THE MIDNIGHT CLEAR...14

JINGLE BELLS...15

JOY TO THE WORLD..16

O COME ALL YE FAITHFUL..17

O COME, O COME EMMANUEL..18

O HOLY NIGHT..19

O LITTLE TOWN OF BETHLEHEM..20

ONCE IN ROYAL DAVID'S CITY..21

SILENT NIGHT..22

THE FIRST NOEL..23

THE HOLLY AND THE IVY..24

THE TWELVE DAYS OF CHRISTMAS..25

UNTO US A CHILD IS BORN..27

WE THREE KINGS..28

WE WISH YOU A MERRY CHRISTMAS..29

WHAT CHILD IS THIS?..31

WHILE SHEPHERDS WATCH THEIR FLOCKS BY NIGHT.......32

Angels from the Realms of Glory

There was with the angel a multitude of the heavenly host praising God, and saying, Glory to God in the highest. Lk. 2:13-14
The desire of all nations shall come: and I will fill this house with glory, saith the Lord of hosts. Hag. 2:7

1. Angels from the realms of glory, Wing your flight o'er all the earth;
   Ye who sang creation's story Now proclaim Messiah's birth.
2. Shepherds, in the field abiding, Watching o'er your flocks by night,
   God with us is now residing; Yonder shines the infant light:
3. Sages, leave your contemplations, Brighter visions beam afar;
   Seek the great Desire of nations; Ye have seen His natal star.
4. Saints, before the altar bending, Watching long in hope and fear;
   Suddenly the Lord, descending, In His temple shall appear.
5. Sinners, wrung with true repentance, Doomed for guilt to endless pains,
   Justice now revokes the sentence, Mercy calls you; break your chains.
6. Though an Infant now we view Him, He shall fill His Father's throne,
   Gather all the nations to Him; Every knee shall then bow down:
7. All creation, join in praising God, the Father, Spirit, Son,
   Evermore your voices raising To th' eternal Three in One.

Refrain
Come and worship, come and worship, Worship Christ, the newborn King.

WORDS: James Montgomery, *pub.* 1816; *v. 5 by* Unknown, *pub.* 1825. MUSIC: "Regent Square"; Henry T. Smart, *pub.* 1867. Public Domain.

Angels We Have Heard on High

Suddenly there was with the angel a multitude of the heavenly host praising God, and saying, Glory to God in the highest, and on earth peace, good will toward men. Lk. 2:13-14

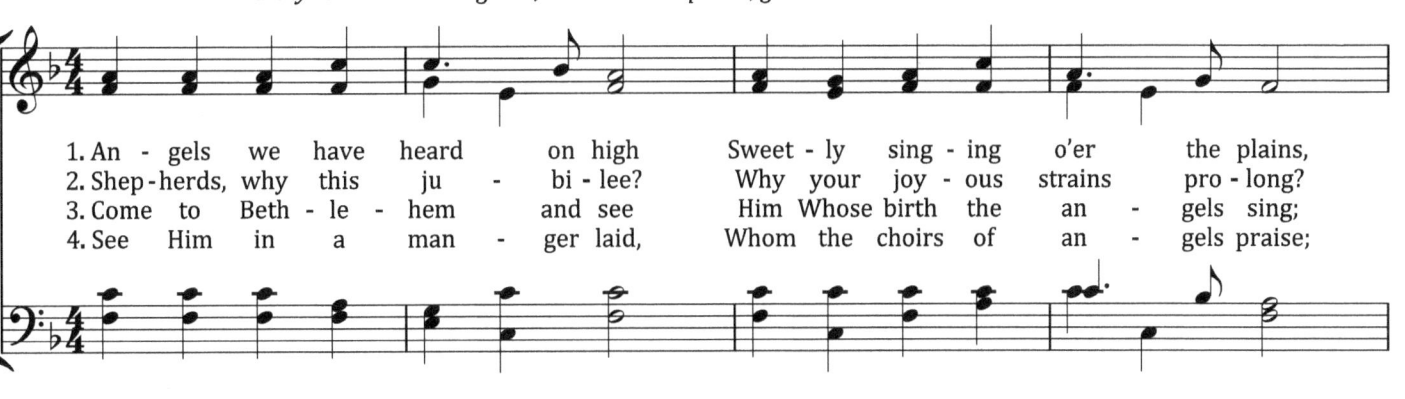

1. Angels we have heard on high Sweetly singing o'er the plains,
2. Shepherds, why this jubilee? Why your joyous strains prolong?
3. Come to Bethlehem and see Him Whose birth the angels sing;
4. See Him in a manger laid, Whom the choirs of angels praise;

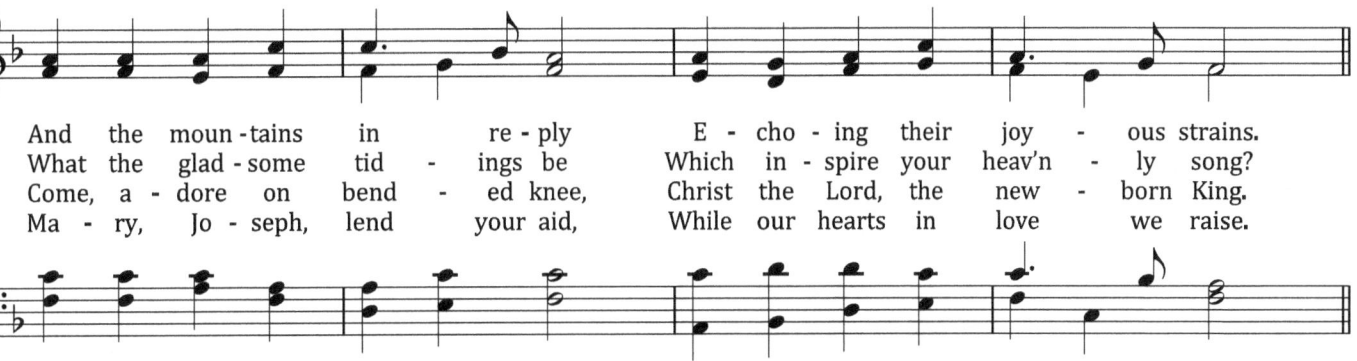

And the mountains in reply Echoing their joyous strains.
What the gladsome tidings be Which inspire your heav'nly song?
Come, adore on bended knee, Christ the Lord, the newborn King.
Mary, Joseph, lend your aid, While our hearts in love we raise.

Refrain

*Glo - - - - - - - ria in excelsis Deo!

Glo - - - - - - - ria in excelsis Deo!

WORDS: Unknown; *tr.* by James Chadwick, *pub.* 1862. MUSIC: "Gloria (Barnes)"; French melody; *arr.* by Edward S. Barnes. Public Domain.
*"Gloria in excelsis Deo" is Latin for "Glory to God in the highest."

As with Gladness Men of Old

The star, which they saw in the east, went before them, till it came and stood over where the young child was. When they saw the star, they rejoiced with exceeding great joy. Mt. 2:9-10

1. As with gladness men of old Did the guiding star behold,
As with joy they hailed its light, Leading onward, beaming bright;
So, most gracious Lord, may we Evermore be led to Thee.

2. As with joyful steps they sped To that lowly manger bed,
There to bend the knee before Him whom heav'n and earth adore;
So may we, with willing feet, Ever seek Thy mercy seat.

3. As they offered gifts most rare At that manger rude and bare;
So may we with holy joy, Pure and free from sin's alloy,
All our costliest treasures bring, Christ, to Thee, our heav'nly King.

4. Holy Jesus, every day Keep us in the narrow way;
And, when earthly things are past, Bring our ransomed souls at last
Where they need no star to guide, Where no clouds Thy glory hide.

WORDS: William C. Dix, *pub.* 1860. MUSIC: "Dix"; Conrad Kocher, 1838; *arr.* by William H. Monk, *pub.* 1861. Public Domain.

Away in a Manger

And she brought forth her firstborn son, and wrapped him in swaddling clothes, and laid him in a manger; because there was no room for them in the inn. Lk. 2:7

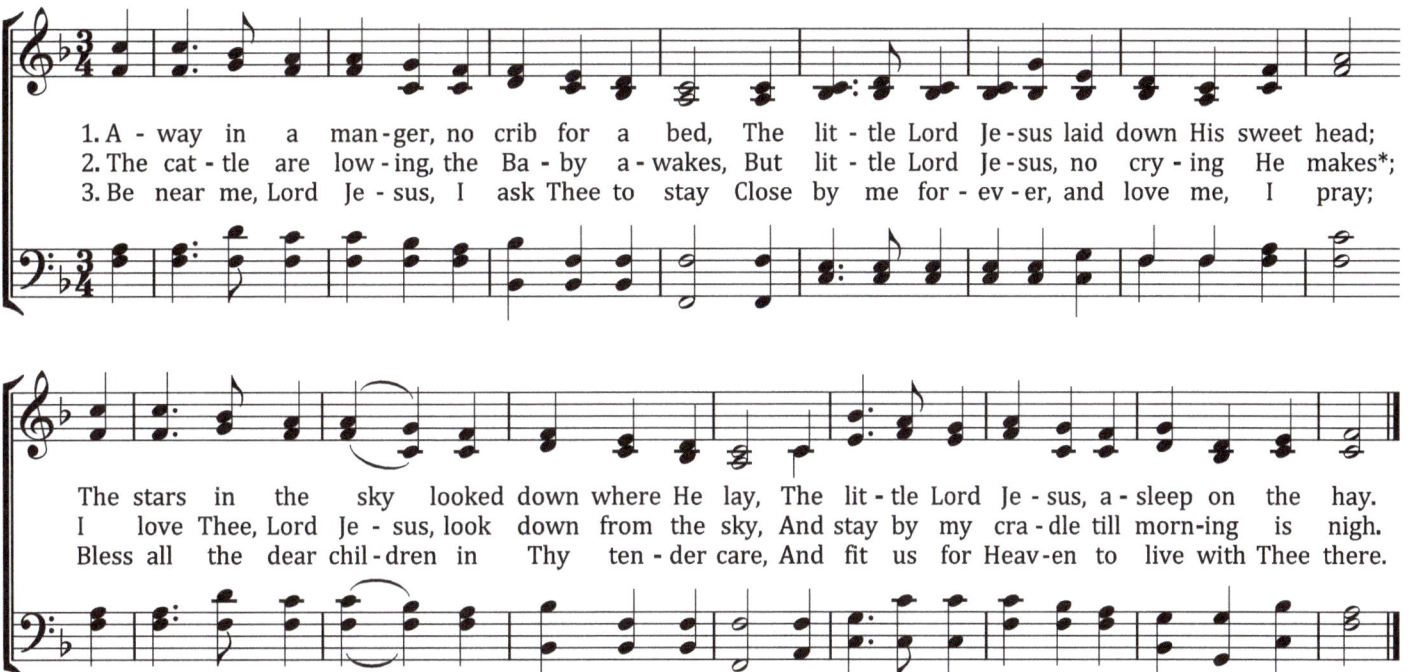

1. A-way in a man-ger, no crib for a bed, The lit-tle Lord Je-sus laid down His sweet head;
2. The cat-tle are low-ing, the Ba-by a-wakes, But lit-tle Lord Je-sus, no cry-ing He makes*;
3. Be near me, Lord Je-sus, I ask Thee to stay Close by me for-ev-er, and love me, I pray;

The stars in the sky looked down where He lay, The lit-tle Lord Je-sus, a-sleep on the hay.
I love Thee, Lord Je-sus, look down from the sky, And stay by my cra-dle till morn-ing is nigh.
Bless all the dear chil-dren in Thy ten-der care, And fit us for Heav-en to live with Thee there.

WORDS: Unknown, *pub.*1885; *v. 3 attr. to* John T. McFarland, *pub.*1892. MUSIC: "Mueller"; James R. Murray, 1887. Public Domain.

*The statement "no crying He makes" is simply a flight of poetic imagination. Scripture teaches that Jesus fully took on human nature, "yet without sin." We have no scriptural authority to imagine that Jesus was the ideal baby. These words should not be viewed as a model of disposition, but only an artistic imagination of the scene at our Savior's birth.

Deck the Halls

words: traditional English

tune: *Nos Galan*, traditional Welsh

Go, Tell It on the Mountain

I bring you good tidings of great joy.... For unto you is born this day in the city of David a Saviour, which is Christ the Lord....
And they... found... the babe lying in a manger. And when they had seen it, they made known abroad the saying. Lk. 2:8-20

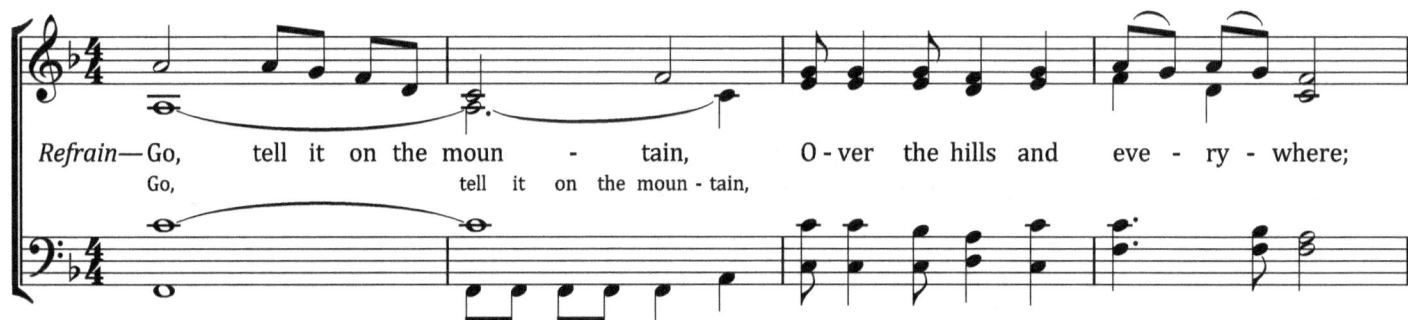

Refrain—Go, tell it on the moun - tain, O - ver the hills and eve - ry - where;
Go, tell it on the moun - tain,

Go, tell it on the moun - tain, That Je - sus Christ is born.
Go, tell it on the moun - tain,

1. While shep - herds kept their watch - ing O'er si - lent flocks by night,
2. The shep - herds feared and trem - bled, When lo! a - bove the earth
3. Down in a low - ly man - ger The hum - ble Christ was born,

Be - hold, through - out the heav - ens There shone a ho - ly light.
Rang out the an - gel cho - rus That hailed the Sav - ior's birth.
And God sent us sal - va - tion That bless - ed Christ - mas morn.

WORDS: Author unknown, *pub.* 1907. MUSIC: "Go Tell It"; African-American melody, *pub.* 1907; *alt.* Public Domain.

Good Christian Men, Rejoice

God so loved the world, that he gave his only begotten Son, that whosoever believeth in him should... have everlasting life. Jn. 3:16
Rejoice greatly, O daughter of Zion... behold, thy King cometh unto thee: he is just, and having salvation. Zec. 9:9; 2:10

1. Good Christian men, rejoice, With heart and soul and voice; Give ye heed to what we say: Jesus Christ is born today; Ox and ass before Him bow; And He is in the manger now. Christ is born today! Christ is born today!
2. Good Christian men, rejoice, With heart and soul and voice; Now ye hear of endless bliss: Jesus Christ was born for this! He has opened heaven's door, And we are blest forevermore. Christ was born for this! Christ was born for this!
3. Good Christian men, rejoice, With heart and soul and voice; Now ye need not fear the grave: Jesus Christ was born to save! Calls you one and calls you all, To gain His everlasting hall. Christ was born to save! Christ was born to save!

WORDS: Author Unknown; *tr. by* John M. Neale, *pub.* 1853. MUSIC: "In Dulci Jubilo"; German melody; *har, pub.* 1871; *alt.,* 1953. Public Domain.

Good King Wenceslas

When thou makest a feast, call the poor, the maimed, the lame, the blind:
And thou shalt be blessed... for thou shalt be recompensed at the resurrection of the just. Lk. 14:13-14

1. Good King Wen-ces-las looked out on the Feast of Ste-phen,
   When the snow lay round a-bout, deep and crisp and e-ven.
   Bright-ly shone the moon that night, though the frost was cru-el,
   When a poor man came in sight, gath-'ring win-ter fu-el.

2. "Hith-er, page, and stand by me, if you know it, tell-ing,
   Yon-der pea-sant, who is he? Where and what his dwell-ing?"
   "Sire, he lives a good league hence, un-der-neath the moun-tain,
   Right a-gainst the for-est fence, by Saint Ag-nes' foun-tain."

3. "Bring me food and bring me wine, bring me pine logs hith-er,
   You and I will see him dine, when we bear them thith-er."
   Page and mon-arch, forth they went, forth they went to-geth-er,
   Through the cold wind's wild la-ment and the bit-ter weath-er.

4. "Sire, the night is dark-er now, and the wind blows strong-er,
   Fails my heart, I know not how; I can go no long-er."
   "Mark my foot-steps, my good page, tread now in them bold-ly,
   You shall find the win-ter's rage freeze your blood less cold-ly."

5. In his mas-ter's steps he trod, where the snow lay dint-ed;
   Heat was in the ver-y sod which the saint had print-ed.
   There-fore, Chris-tian men, be sure, while God's gifts pos-sess-ing,
   You who now will bless the poor shall your-selves find bless-ing.

WORDS: John M. Neale, *pub.* 1853; *alt.* MUSIC: "Tempus Adest Floridum"; Swedish melody, *pub.* 1582. Public Domain.

I Heard the Bells on Christmas Day

*There was with the angel a multitude of the heavenly host praising God, and saying,
Glory to God in the highest, and on earth peace, good will toward men.* Lk. 2:13-14; Rom. 5:1

1. I heard the bells on Christmas day Their old familiar carols play; In music sweet the tones repeat, "There's peace on earth, good will to men."
2. I thought how, as the day had come, The belfries of all Christendom Had rolled along th' unbroken song Of peace on earth, good will to men.
3. And in despair I bowed my head: "There is no peace on earth," I said, "For hate is strong, and mocks the song Of peace on earth, good will to men."
4. Then pealed the bells more loud and deep: "God is not dead, nor does He sleep, For Christ is here; His Spirit near Brings peace on earth, good will to men."
5. When men repent and turn from sin The Prince of Peace then enters in, And grace imparts within their hearts His peace on earth, good will to men.
6. O souls amid earth's busy strife, The Word of God is light and life; Oh, hear His voice, make Him your choice, Hail peace on earth, good will to men.
7. Then happy, singing on your way, Your world will change from night to day; Your heart will feel the message real, Of peace on earth, good will to men.

WORDS: Henry W. Longfellow, 1864; *alt. and v. 5-7 by* Harlan D. Sorrell. MUSIC: "Waltham"; John B. Calkin, 1872. Public Domain.

I Saw Three Ships

Traditional

2. And what was in those ships all three?
   On Christmas day, on Christmas day,
   And what was in those ships all three?
   On Christmas day in the morning.

3. The Virgin Mary and Christ were there,
   On Christmas day, on Christmas day,
   The Virgin Mary and Christ were there,
   On Christmas day in the morning.

4. Pray wither sailed those ships all three?
   On Christmas day, on Christmas day,
   Pray wither sailed those ships all three?
   On Christmas day in the morning.

5. Oh, they sailed into Bethlehem,
   On Christmas day, on Christmas day,
   Oh, they sailed into Bethlehem,
   On Christmas day in the morning.

6. And all the bells on earth shall ring,
   On Christmas day, on Christmas day,
   And all the bells on earth shall ring,
   On Christmas day in the morning.

7. And all the Angels in Heaven shall sing,
   On Christmas day, on Christmas day,
   And all the Angels in Heaven shall sing,
   On Christmas day in the morning.

8. And all the souls on earth shall sing,
   On Christmas day, on Christmas day,
   And all the souls on earth shall sing,
   On Christmas day in the morning.

9. Then let us all rejoice, amain,
   On Christmas day, on Christmas day,
   Then let us all rejoice, amain,
   On Christmas day in the morning.

This work is in the Public Domain. For more free sheet music visit www.cantorion.org
Music engraving by LilyPond 2.11.38—www.lilypond.org

Joy to the World

*The angel said unto them, Fear not: for, behold,
I bring you good tidings of great joy, which shall be to all people.* Lk. 2:10

1. Joy to the world, the Lord is come! Let earth re-ceive her King;
2. Joy to the earth, the Sav-ior reigns! Let men their songs em-ploy;
3. No more let sins and sor-rows grow, Nor thorns in-fest the ground;
4. He rules the world with truth and grace, And makes the na-tions prove

Let eve-ry heart pre-pare Him room,
While fields and floods, rocks, hills, and plains
He comes to make His bless-ings flow
The glo-ries of His right-eous-ness,

And heav'n and na-ture sing, And heav'n and na-ture sing,
Re-peat the sound-ing joy, Re-peat the sound-ing joy,
Far as the curse is found, Far as the curse is found,
And won-ders of His love, And won-ders of His love,

(1) And heav'n and na-ture sing, And heav'n and na-

And heav'n, and heav'n, and na-ture sing.
Re-peat, re-peat, the sound-ing joy.
Far as, far as, the curse is found.
And won-ders, won-ders, of His love.

ture sing,

WORDS: Isaac Watts, *pub.* 1719. MUSIC: "Antioch"; George F. Handel; *arr.* by Lowell Mason, *pub.* 1836. Public Domain.

Oh, Come, All Ye Faithful

The shepherds said one to another, Let us now go even unto Bethlehem, and see this thing which is come to pass....
And they came with haste, and found Mary, and Joseph, and the babe lying in a manger. Lk. 2:15-16

1. Oh, come, all ye faithful, joyful and triumphant,
   Oh, come ye, oh, come ye, to Bethlehem.
   Come and behold Him, born the King of angels;
2. Sing, choirs of angels, sing in exultation,
   Oh, sing, all ye citizens of heav'n above!
   Glory to God, all glory in the highest;
3. Yea, Lord, we greet Thee, born this happy morning;
   Jesus, to Thee be all glory giv'n;
   Word of the Father, now in flesh appearing;

Refrain
Oh, come, let us adore Him, oh, come, let us adore Him,
Oh, come, let us adore Him, Christ the Lord.

WORDS: John F. Wade, *ca.*1743; v. 1-2 tr. by Frederick Oakeley, 1841. MUSIC: "Adeste Fideles"; J. F. W., *ca.*1743. Public Domain.

O Come, O Come, Emmanuel

The Lord himself shall give you a sign; shall... bear a son, and shall call his name Immanuel. Isa. 7:14; Mt. 1:21-23
I will shake all nations, and the desire of all nations shall come: and I will fill this house with glory, saith the Lord of hosts. Hag. 2:7

1. O come, O come, Emmanuel, And ransom captive Israel
That mourns in lonely exile here, Until the Son of God appear.

2. O come, Thou Wisdom from on high, Who orders all things mightily;
To us the path of knowledge show, And teach us in its ways to go.

3. O come, Thou Branch of Jesse's stem, Unto Thine own and rescue them!
From depths of hell Thy people save, And give them vict'ry o'er the grave.

4. O come, Thou Key of David, come And open wide our heav'nly home;
Make safe for us the heav'nward road, And bar the way to death's abode.

5. O come, Thou Bright and Morning Star, And bring us comfort from afar!
Dispel the shadows of the night And turn our darkness into light.

6. O come, Desire of nations, bind In one the hearts of all mankind;
Bid all our sad divisions cease, And be Thyself our King of Peace.

Refrain
Rejoice! Rejoice! Emmanuel Shall come to thee, O Israel.

WORDS: Latin chant, *12th cent.*; *tr. by* John M. Neale, *pub.*1851; *v. 2, 6 tr. attr. to* Henry S. Coffin; *alt.*
MUSIC: "Veni Emmanuel"; French melody; *arr. by* Thomas Helmore, *pub.*1856. Public Domain.

Once in Royal David's City

Cecil Frances Humphreys Alexander — Henry John Gauntlett

1. Once in roy-al Da-vid's ci-ty Stood a low-ly cat-tle shed, Where a Mo-ther laid her Ba-by In a man-ger for His bed; Ma-ry was that Mo-ther mild, Je-sus Christ her on-ly Child

2. He came down to earth from Heaven,
   Who is God and Lord of all,
   And His shelter was a stable,
   And His cradle was a Stall;
   With the poor, and mean and lowly,
   Lived on earth our Saviour holy.

3. And through all His wondrous Childhood,
   He would honour and obey,
   Love and watch the lowly Maiden,
   In whose gentle arms He lay;
   Christian children all must be
   Mild, obedient, good, as He.

4. For He is our childhood's pattern,
   Day by day like us He grew,
   He was little, weak, and helpless,
   Fears and smiles like us He knew,
   And He feeleth for our sadness,
   And He shareth in our gladness.

5. And our eyes at last shall see Him,
   Through His own redeeming love,
   For that Child, so dear and gentle,
   Is our Lord in Heaven above;
   And He leads His children on
   To the place where He is gone.

6. Not in that poor lowly stable,
   With the oxen standing by,
   We shall see Him; but in Heaven,
   Set at God's right Hand on High;
   When like sars His children crowned,
   All in white, shall wait around.

This work is in the Public Domain. For more free sheet music visit www.cantorion.org
Music engraving by LilyPond 2.11.38—www.lilypond.org

Silent Night

There were in the same country shepherds... keeping watch over their flock by night. And, lo, the angel of the Lord came upon them, and the glory of the Lord shone round about them.... And they came with haste, and found... the babe lying in a manger. Lk. 2:8-9,16

1. Si - lent night, ho - ly night! All is calm, all is bright
2. Si - lent night, ho - ly night! Shep - herds quake at the sight;
3. Si - lent night, ho - ly night! Son of God, love's pure light
4. Si - lent night, ho - ly night! Won - drous star, lend thy light;

Round yon vir - gin moth - er and Child. Ho - ly In - fant, so ten - der and mild,
Glo - ries stream from heav - en a - far, Heav'n - ly hosts sing Al - le - lu - ia!
Ra - diant beams from Thy ho - ly face With the dawn of re - deem - ing grace,
With the an - gels let us sing, Al - le - lu - ia to our King;

Sleep in heav - en - ly peace, Sleep in heav - en - ly peace.
Christ the Sav - ior is born, Christ the Sav - ior is born!
Je - sus, Lord, at Thy birth, Je - sus, Lord, at Thy birth.
Christ the Sav - ior is born, Christ the Sav - ior is born!

WORDS: Josef Mohr, *ca.1817*; *vs. 1,3 tr. by* John F. Young, 1863; *vs. 2,4 tr. by* Anonymous. MUSIC: "Stille Nacht"; Franz X. Gruber, *ca.1820.* Public Domain.

The Holly and the Ivy

Traditional

1. The Hol-ly and the I-vy Now both are full well grown, Of all the trees that are in the wood, The Hol-ly bears the crown.
2. The Hol-ly bears a blos-som, As white as lil-y-flower; And Ma-ry bore sweet Je-sus Christ, To be our sweet Sav-ior.
3. The Hol-ly bears a ber-ry, As red as an-y blood; And Ma-ry bore sweet Je-sus Christ, To do poor sin-ners good.
4. The Hol-ly bears a prick-le, As sharp as an-y thorn; And Ma-ry bore sweet Je-sus Christ, On Christ-mas Day in the morn.
5. The Hol-ly bears a bark, As bit-ter as an-y gall; And Ma-ry bore sweet Je-sus Christ, For to re-deem us all.
6. The Hol-ly and the I-vy Now both are full well grown, Of all the trees that are in the wood, The Hol-ly bears the crown.

Refrain: O the ris-ing of the sun, The run-ning of the deer, The play-ing of the mer-ry or-gan, Sweet sing-ing in the quire, Sweet sing-ing in the quire.

Public Domain
Courtesy of the Cyber Hymnal™

The Twelve Days of Christmas

Traditional English

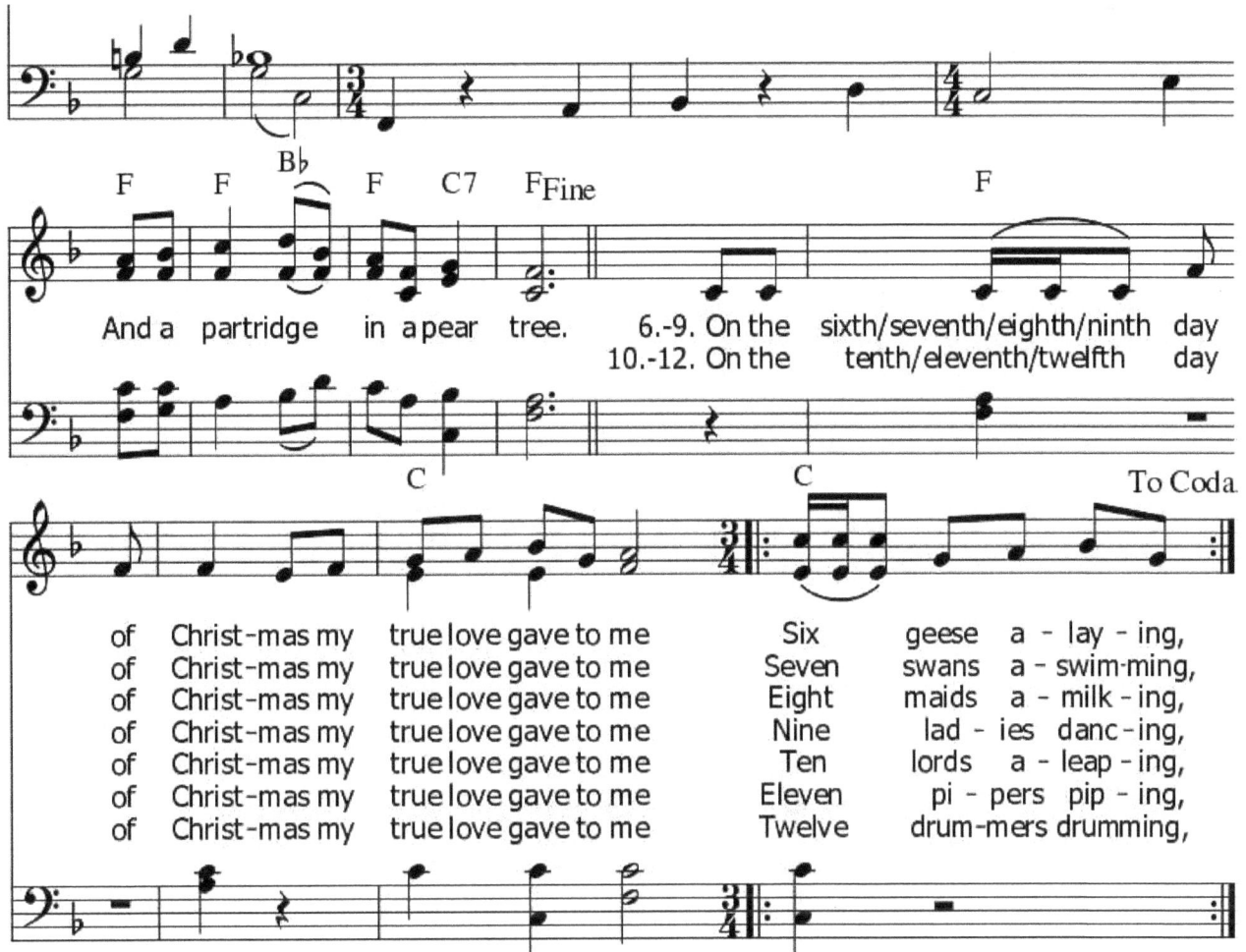

Unto Us a Child is Born

Trier, Germany, 15th Century

Public Domain
Courtesy of the Cyber Hymnal™

We Three Kings of Orient Are

When Jesus was born in Bethlehem of Judaea in the days of Herod the king, behold, there came wise men from the east to Jerusalem,
Saying, Where is he that is born King of the Jews? for we have seen his star in the east, and are come to worship him. Mt. 2:1-2

1. We three* kings of O-ri-ent are; Bear-ing gifts we tra-verse a-far,
2. Born a King on Beth-le-hem's plain Gold I bring to crown Him a-gain,
3. Fran-kin-cense to of-fer have I; In-cense owns a De-i-ty nigh;
4. Myrrh is mine, its bit-ter per-fume Breathes a life of gath-er-ing gloom;
5. Glo-rious now be-hold Him a-rise; King and God and sac-ri-fice;

Field and foun-tain, moor and moun-tain, Fol-low-ing yon-der star.
King for-ev-er, ceas-ing nev-er, O-ver us all to reign.
Prayer and prais-ing, voic-es rais-ing, Wor-ship-ing God on high.
Sor-r'wing, sigh-ing, bleed-ing, dy-ing, Sealed in the stone cold tomb.
Al-le-lu-ia, A-le-lu-ia, Sounds thro' the earth and skies.

Refrain

O star of won-der, star of night, Star with roy-al beau-ty bright,
West-ward lead-ing, still pro-ceed-ing, Guide us to thy per-fect light.

WORDS and MUSIC: "Kings of Orient"; John H. Hopkins, Jr., 1857. Public Domain.

*The Bible mentions three gifts, but does not state the number of wise men.

We Wish You a Merry Christmas

Traditional English

What Child Is This?

...And she brought forth her firstborn son, and wrapped him in swaddling clothes, and laid him in a manger; because there was no room for them in the inn. Lk. 2:7

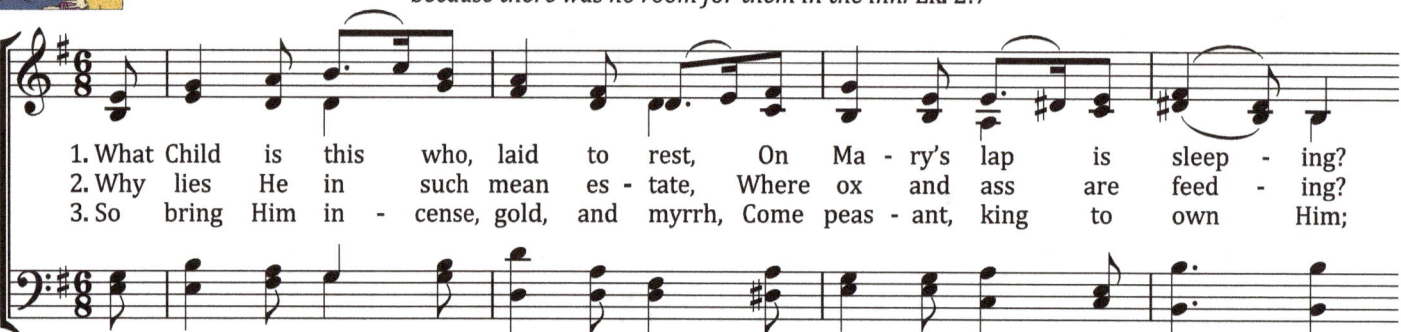

1. What Child is this who, laid to rest, On Mary's lap is sleeping?
2. Why lies He in such mean estate, Where ox and ass are feeding?
3. So bring Him incense, gold, and myrrh, Come peasant, king to own Him;

Whom angels greet with anthems sweet, While shepherds watch are keeping?
Good Christians, fear, for sinners here The silent Word is pleading.
The King of kings salvation brings, Let loving hearts enthrone Him.

This, this is Christ the King, Whom shepherds guard and angels sing;
Nails, spear shall pierce Him through, The cross be borne for me, for you;
Raise, raise a song on high, The virgin sings her lullaby;

Haste, haste to bring Him laud, The Babe, the Son of Mary.
Hail, hail the Word made flesh, The Babe, the Son of Mary.
Joy, joy for Christ is born, The Babe, the Son of Mary.

WORDS: William C. Dix, *pub.* 1865. MUSIC: "Greensleeves"; English melody. Public Domain.

While Shepherds Watched Their Flocks

There were in the same country shepherds abiding in the field, keeping watch over their flock by night.
And, lo, the angel of the Lord came upon them, and the glory of the Lord shone round about them. Lk. 2:8-9

1. While shep-herds watched their flocks by night, All seat-ed on the ground, The an-gel of the Lord came down, And glo-ry shone a-round, And glo-ry shone a-round.
2. "Fear not!" said he, for might-y dread Had seized their trou-bled mind; "Glad tid-ings of great joy I bring To you and all man-kind, To you and all man-kind.
3. "To you, in Da-vid's town, this day Is born of Da-vid's line A Sav-ior, who is Christ the Lord, All mean-ly wrapped in swath-ing bands, And this shall be the sign, And this shall be the sign:
4. "The heav'n-ly Babe you there shall find To hu-man view dis-played, All mean-ly wrapped in swath-ing bands, And in a man-ger laid, And in a man-ger laid."
5. Thus spake the ser-aph and forth-with Ap-peared a shin-ing throng Of an-gels prais-ing God on high, Who thus ad-dressed their song, Who thus ad-dressed their song:
6. "All glo-ry be to God on high, And to the Earth be peace; Good will hence-forth from heav'n to men Be-gin and nev-er cease, Be-gin and nev-er cease!"

WORDS: Nahum Tate, 1700. MUSIC: "Christmas"; George F. Handel, 1728; *arr., pub.* 1812. Public Domain.

www.ingramcontent.com/pod-product-compliance
Lightning Source LLC
LaVergne TN
LVHW060221080526
838202LV00052B/4322